8 Steps to Embrace Your Well-Being

CLAIM YOUR CONFIDENCE NOW

ROSALES MAVERICKS™ PUBLISHING STUDIO

I invite you to watch this video before you begin your Claim Your Confidence NOW Workbook

Title: CLAIM YOUR CONFIDENCE NOW
Subtitle: 8 Steps to Embrace Your Well-Being
ISBN: 978-1-959471-02-8 (English Paperback)

Categories: Performance Arts, Dance, Personal Development
Cover design by: RMPStudio™
Team Editor: RMPStudio™ Team
Printed in the United States of America
Photographers: Margaryta Mosina and Sarah Banch
Wellness Contributors: www.lasvegasholisticcenter.com, www.freshstartnb.com

ORDERING INFORMATION: www.GinaPero.com

Publisher: Rosales Mavericks Publishing Studio™ (RMPStudio™) 1180 N. Town Center Suite #100, Las Vegas, Nevada 89144

Your dancing soul is here for a purpose.

YOUR

8

STEPS

TO EMBRACE YOUR
WELL-BEING

You are invited on a journey of self-discovery.

Foreword

We are living in a world that not only challenges our sense of self-esteem yet enhances our doubts and worries. The journey of discovering our self confidence can be intimidating. Yet, Gina has crafted a motivational path that blocks out the stresses of the outside world and teaches us how to let your light shine through all darknesses. It is with great honor that I write this foreword for Gina Pero's inspiring workbook, "Claim Your Confidence NOW."

This book teaches readers of all ages how to transform into the best version of themselves, and how to stray away from self-doubt and all insecurities. This is a workbook that allows young individuals to stand tall and confident in their unique values. Gina provides a roadmap that helps to achieve one's highest potential, admire themselves, and live a happy and heart healthy life.

As a dancer and someone who has spent the past few years working on my well-being and self-appreciation, I am deeply moved by the care behind each word Gina provides on each page. Her passion for empowering young minds is a beacon of light, offering the most uplifting experience for her readers.

To the readers of "Claim Your Confidence NOW," I encourage you to embrace this wonderful journey wholeheartedly. With Gina's intelligence and determination there are no limits on your dreams, no mountain you cannot move, and no words that can break you down.

Warm Regards,
Ema Flannery, Performing Artist, The Peroettes Program

Your
path to
well-being
is here.

Wellness Contributors

Dr. David Stella

Dr. David A. Stella has been a Chiropractor in Las Vegas, NV since 1998. He has a special interest in functional and energy medicine with a love for teaching people what is highest and best for their own individual bodies and how they can tap into their own wisdom. Having a daughter who grew up dancing and graduated with a dance degree, Dr. Stella has compassion and understands what the life of a dancer looks, feels, and sounds like. He is the owner of The Las Vegas Holistic Center with a mission to guide people to extraordinary health and well-being.

Karen Turnbull

Karen Turnbull has spent 20+ years working with dancers to help bring them into their best mobility, balance, and health so they can achieve their best performances. Her experience as a professional dancer, dance educator, and choreographer transitioned her into a massage therapist, myofascial stretch therapist, and certified nutrition coach after recognizing her passion for health was to help others too. Her mission is to guide dancers of all ages and levels into their most optimal full body balance and health so they feel at their best daily.

Love
yourself just as
you are at this
moment.

Introduction

"I allow the light of the universe to move through me today, bringing to life my most fulfilling reality, for the well-being of all that I am now, and so it is....with ease and with joy."

Each morning I awake, this is part of my morning ritual. Ever since I was a young dancer, I knew the moment I stepped on the stage, my spirit felt alive. It was one of the most fulfilling experiences I feel so blessed to have witnessed.

Growing up in a small town, and wearing a back brace for scoliosis during the ages of twelve to sixteen, I became aware of the power of "choice." Do I wear my back brace when I dance or when I sleep?

This was one of the easiest decisions for me at that time, knowing how much I enjoyed the art of dance. Dance plays many roles in my life, and I wonder the roles it plays for you. At times, it offers my high achieving soul a chance to feel stretched. At times, it creates a sense of belonging. At times, it is the "spoonful of sugar," that Mary Poppins talks about, that helps the medicine go down. I decided young, that dance had a purpose, and I knew that the purpose would change from time to time.

You see the word "confidence," was not at the center of my thoughts growing up. I focused on what I enjoyed the most, and I knew that when I began to enjoy something else, I would change my direction. (We call that a pivot, in dance class.)

Confidence, dear readers, is a pathway, another word can be process. You can choose the steps each day to arrive at the destination you want to grow to, not get to.

This workbook provides you with simple processes towards eight specific pathways to your unique style of well-being. Well-being can be different for each of you. It is created by you and for you, as you decide this is what you want.

Introduction

A question I was asked in becoming a certified coach was, "What do you want to do with your one precious life."

My dear dance artists, you get to decide what and how dance plays a role on your path. You get to choose how you want to think, how you want to feel, and how you want to act. You get to enjoy what you decide lights your spirit up. Whether it's onstage or offstage, you choose what you accept in your mind, your body, and your soul.

There is a saying that begins with "Repetition is the mother of learning...."

What you think on repeat, say on repeat, and do on repeat creates your reality. In this workbook, you will learn the tools to practice daily that can lead you to your extraordinary life.

When I lived in Italy, I learned a saying, " grazie mille", a thousand thanks.

I want to thank my family, friends, teachers, colleagues, students, clients, The Peroettes, all of my dance experiences, and the power of the Universe, which I call, God. Each of you have played your role along my path, and I am grateful for your timing in showing up. To my publisher, you are a rockstar! To my love David, you are my healing balm.

To all of you readers, I thank you for choosing your path to well-being. Thank you for choosing dance as a pathway in your life.

Together we get to create whatever we repeat in our mind, our body, and our soul.

Grazie Mille,
Your Loving Guide, Gina

Directions

Each page has a pathway that guides you through a process so you can discover what your personal 'style' is for each step towards self-confidence and well-being.

Definition

You will be able to read a definition of each step and then be asked to write it in your own words. This allows you to feel connected and clearer in your own self-understanding of what it is for you at this present time.

Self-Assessment

Self-Assessments use empowering questions with a scaling process to help you identify where you are today and a specific way you can slide along the scale.

Professional Tips

Professional Tips guide you with an idea, an exercise, and or a tool from one of our wellness contributors.

Self-Caring

Gina provides three specific ways that she uses self-caring techniques for each step offering you examples that can inspire your own self-caring techniques.

Directions

Self-Awareness

Self-Awareness has the question to clarify how you see yourself, hear yourself, and know yourself

Self-Reflection

Self-Reflection is a process for you to evaluate yourself and your answers. This process helps you decide how you want to retain, what you have learned.

Self-Reminders

Reminders are created to enhance your memory. Your retention style can be visual, audio, kinesthetic, verbal, writing, and/or teaching.

Examples: Set an alarm on a device with the exact reminder at a certain time. Use a post it note to write what you want to remember. Audio record yourself and listen to it. Share what you learn with someone. Take notes. Take action on the new things you want to remember and repeat.

Acknowledgment

Gina will acknowledge you after you complete each step.
Take time to fully receive the message.

Table of Contents

Are you ready to turn your light up!?

Restful
Sleep

1

Restful
Sleep

Dear Dancer,

I know what it's like to be a high performing artist, and still feel emotionally and physically exhausted, as your schedule keeps you in 24/7 performance mode.

I know what it's like to think about when and how one would get rest adequately, as you want to fit everything in and still feel your best.

I also know that as you discover what restful sleep is for you in the following pages, you will begin to raise your energy and confidence.

You will start to notice how simple your restful sleep choreography can be, and how easy it is to implement.

I know in this moment, you are here for a higher purpose, and I know you will practice this restful sleep choreography so you will perform your best in mind, body, and spirit.

So, are you ready to turn the page and step onto the well-being stage? A 5678...

Gina

Restful Sleep

Restful Sleep is a vital component of optimal health and well-being. It is necessary to reset your nervous system, recover, and heal itself.

Fill in the blank:

Restful sleep for me is...

Self-Assessment

On a scale of 1–10, 10 being the best, color in the number that reflects your understanding of what restful sleep is right now?

What is a specific action you can choose that will encourage you to move forward to the next number?

On a scale of 1–10, 10 being the best, color in the number that reflects your restful sleep right now?

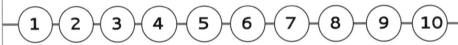

What is a specific action you can choose that will encourage you to move forward to the next number?

On a scale of 1–10, 10 being the best, color in the number that reflects your willingness to learn about your restful sleep?

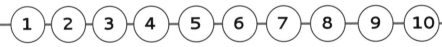

What is a specific action you can choose that will encourage you to move forward to the next number?

Professional Tips

Dr. Stella

No Technology within 15 feet your bed

Clean air, no artificial fresheners, and choose unscented bedding

Karen Turnbull

No screen time before bed, choose to color, meditate, stretch, or read

Write down three things you are grateful for that day

Self-Caring

Gina's Self-Caring Shares

- Before bed I choose to turn off technology 30-60 minutes prior

- Before Bed I choose to do my stretch and breathwork practice

- In bed, I choose to name what I am grateful for , remind myself of what I have in my life, and pray

Next to each bullet, fill in the blank

- Before Bed I choose

- Before Bed I choose

- In Bed I choose

Self-Awareness

What is one thing you learned about yourself after taking the self-assessment?

What is one specific skill or action from your self-assessment that you will implement today?

What professional tip will you begin to use?

What will you choose from the self caring worksheet to take action on?

What will your life look, feel, and sound like if you decide to use your self-awareness tools?

Self-Reflection

What do you know now about your restful sleep that
you did not know before this workbook?

On a scale of 1–10, 10 being the best, color in the number that
best reflects your confidence now about your restful sleep?

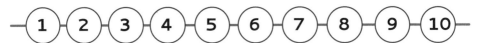

What is a specific skill or action you will begin to practice for
your restful sleep?

What reminder will encourage you to remember what restful
sleep is for you?

What do you appreciate about yourself after learning about
your restful sleep?

Reminders

Create your reminders below

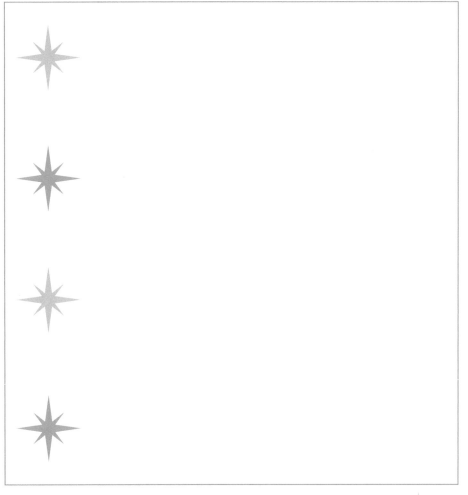

I acknowledge you today
for your dedication.
You learned what restful sleep is
for the well-being of your mind,
body, and spirit.
I invite you to appreciate yourself
right now, in this moment.
As you begin to implement this new
choreography into your daily
routine, know how grateful your
body feels and what else is
possible for you right now.

Shine On

Gina

Mindful Hydration

Dear Dancer,

I know what it's like to be a high performing artist, and still feel burnt out and stressed – even if you think you "should" love dance all of the time.

I know what it's like to think about when and how one would get adequate amounts of water, as you want to grasp every lesson in the classroom, putting your bladder on hold.

I also know that as you discover what mindful hydration is in the following pages, you will begin to raise your water bottle and laugh out loud at how you can water your mind and body so easily.

You will start to notice how simple your mindful hydration choreography can be, and how easy it is to implement, even inside the classroom.

I know in this moment, you are here for your love of dance, and I know you will practice this mindful hydration choreography right away.

So, are you ready to turn the page and step onto the well–being stage? A 5678...

Gina

Mindful Hydration

Mindful hydration is being aware of
your daily water intake

Fill in the blank:

Mindful Hydration for me is...

Self-Assessment

On a scale of 1–10, 10 being the best, color in the number that reflects your understanding of what mindful hydration is right now?

What is a specific action you can choose that will encourage you to move forward to the next number?

On a scale of 1–10, 10 being the best, color in the number that reflects your mindful hydration right now?

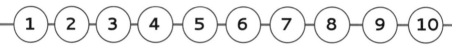

What is a specific action you can choose that will encourage you to move forward to the next number?

On a scale of 1–10, 10 being the best, color in the number that reflects your willingness to learn about your mindful hydration?

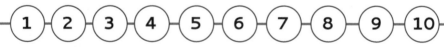

What is a specific action you can choose that will encourage you to move forward to the next number?

Professional Tips

Dr. Stella

Drink at least half your body weight in ounces.
Example: If you are 120 lbs then drink 60 ounces
of water.

Remember, your body is made up of 70% water, so
it loves water to function properly.

Karen Turnbull

Find a water bottle you love!

Hydrate your body! Feeling tight and sore can be
a sign of dehydration.

Self-Caring

Gina's Self-Caring Shares

- I have a morning routine of drinking the glass of water I leave on my bathroom counter

- I focus on my mineral intake daily to maintain balance in my body

- I have reminders set in my phone to remind me to drink water and check in with my minerals

Next to each bullet, fill in the blank

- I drink water when

- I make sure I have

- I have

Self-Awareness

What is one thing you learned about yourself after taking the self-assessment?

What is one specific skill or action from your self-assessment that you will implement today?

What professional tip will you begin to use?

What will you choose from the self caring worksheet to take action on?

What will your life look, feel, and sound like if you decide to use your self-awareness tools?

Self-Reflection

What do you know now about your mindful hydration that you did not know before this workbook?

On a scale of 1-10, 10 being the best, color in the number that best reflects your confidence now about your mindful hydration?

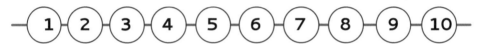

What is a specific skill or action you will begin to practice for your mindful hydration?

What reminder will encourage you to remember what mindful hydration is to you?

What do you appreciate about yourself after learning about your mindful hydration?

Reminders

Create your reminders below

*I acknowledge you
today for your courage.
You learned what mindful
hydration is for the well-being of
your mind, body, and spirit.
I invite you to appreciate yourself
right now, in this moment.
As you begin to implement this new
choreography into your daily
routine, know how grateful your
body feels and what else is
possible for you right now.*

Shine On

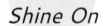

Empowered
Heart

Dear Dancer,

I know what it's like to be a high performing artist, and at times, fall out of love with your art, because you can't seem to live up to the standards you set for yourself and perfectionista is running the show!

I know what it's like to think about when and how one would have enough time to easily let go of judgements and expectations and listen more to your empowered heart, and choose self-love over self-fear.

I also know that as you discover what an empowered heart is in the following pages, you will begin to ignite your self-awareness and follow your heart more easily.

You will start to notice how simple your empowered heart choreography can be, and how easy it is to implement, even when you feel stressed.

I know in this moment, you are here to get to know your empowered heart, and I know you when you know, your empowered heart practice will become permanent.

So, are you ready to turn the page and step onto the well-being stage? A 5678...

Gina

Empowered Heart

An Empowered Heart is tuning in to your hearts contents knowing what moves you and lights you up, mentally, physically, spiritually, and emotionally.

Fill in the blank:

Empowered Heart for me is...

Self-Assessment

On a scale of 1–10, 10 being the best, color in the number that reflects your understanding of what empowered heart is right now?

What is a specific action you can choose that will encourage you to move forward to the next number?

On a scale of 1–10, 10 being the best, color in the number that reflects your empowered heart right now?

What is a specific action you can choose that will encourage you to move forward to the next number?

On a scale of 1–10, 10 being the best, color in the number that reflects your willingness to learn about your empowered heart?

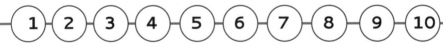

What is a specific action you can choose that will encourage you to move forward to the next number?

Professional Tips

Dr. Stella

Say, "Today I choose me first to love, honor and nurture"

Ask the universe, "Show me what unconditional love looks like, feels like, sounds like at home, school, and dance."

Karen Turnbull

The heart is an amazing muscle! Exercise it with cardio movements you enjoy.

Deep breathing

Self-Caring

Gina's Self-Caring Shares

- Before I get out of bed I place my hands on my heart, take a deep breath, and say how grateful I am for my body., my health, and my life.
- I choose my favorite exercise throughout the day to encourage my heart, by inhaling through the nose, holding it for two, and exhaling slowly through my mouth
- I fuel my body, mind, and soul with things I love

Next to each bullet, fill in the blank

- I choose

- I strengthen my heart by

- I fuel my body, mind, and soul with

Self-Awareness

What is one thing you learned about yourself after taking the self-assessment?

What is one specific skill or action from your self-assessment that you will implement today?

What professional tip will you begin to use?

What will you choose from the self caring worksheet to take action on?

What will your life look, feel, and sound like if you decide to use your self-awareness tools?

Self-Reflection

What do you know now about your empowered heart
that you did not know before this workbook?

On a scale of 1–10, 10 being the best, color in the number that
best reflects your confidence now about your empowered heart?

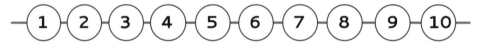

What is a specific skill or action you will begin to practice for
your empowered heart?

What reminder will encourage you to remember what
empowers your heart?

What do you appreciate about yourself after learning about
your empowered heart?

Reminders

Create your reminders below

I acknowledge you today
for your loving awareness.
You learned what an empowered
heart is for the well–being of your
mind, body, and spirit.
I invite you to appreciate yourself
right now, in this moment.
As you begin to implement this
new choreography into your daily
routine, know how grateful your
body feels and what else is
possible for you right now.

Shine On

Gina

Universal
Support

Dear Dancer,

   I know what it's like to be a high performing artist, and at times feel isolated and disconnected from your loved ones and universal support, because you think "I'm too busy" or "I've just gotta finish..."or " I don't fit in."

   I know what it's like to think about when and how one would be more present and connected, knowing that support is everywhere.

   I also know that as you discover what universal support is in the following pages, you will begin to understand that you have exactly what you need to feel connected all the time.

   You will start to notice how simple your universal support choreography can be, and how easy it is to implement, even when you are alone.

   I know at this moment, you are here to get to know what universal support is for you and how to access it wherever you are in the world.

    So, are you ready to turn the page and step onto the well-being stage? A 5678...

Gina

Universal Support

The Universe is supporting you, fueling your mind, body and spirit with the people, places, and things that elevate you and your life journey

Fill in the blank:

Universal Support for me is...

Self-Assessment

On a scale of 1–10, 10 being the best, color in the number that reflects your understanding of what universal support is right now?

What is a specific action you can choose that will encourage you to move forward to the next number?

On a scale of 1–10, 10 being the best, color in the number that reflects your universal support right now?

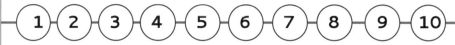

What is a specific action you can choose that will encourage you to move forward to the next number?

On a scale of 1–10, 10 being the best, color in the number that reflects your willingness to learn about your universal support?

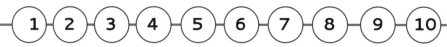

What is a specific action you can choose that will encourage you to move forward to the next number?

Professional Tips

Dr. Stella

Nourish your body with whole foods so it can function at its highest and best

Ask for assistance, ask for direction, ask and you shall receive

Karen Turnbull

Evaluate your social environment by naming the people who light you up and make you feel excited about your day

Declutter your surroundings! Your environmental health matters.

Self-Caring

Gina's Self-Caring Shares

- I connect with three supportive and loving family and friends each day

- I choose people, places, and things that empower and energize me

- I personally support myself with my daily prayers and communication with my guides

Next to each bullet, fill in the blank

- I connect with

- I choose people places and things that

- I personally support myself by

Self-Awareness

What is one thing you learned about yourself after taking the self-assessment?

What is one specific skill or action from your self-assessment that you will implement today?

What professional tip will you begin to use?

What will you choose from the self caring worksheet to take action on?

What will your life look, feel, and sound like if you decide to use your self-awareness tools?

Self-Reflection

What do you know now about your universal support
that you did not know before this workbook?

On a scale of 1-10, 10 being the best, color in the number that
best reflects your confidence now about your universal support?

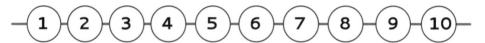

1 2 3 4 5 6 7 8 9 10

What is a specific skill or action you will begin to practice for
your universal support?

What reminder will encourage you to remember what
universally supports you?

What do you appreciate about yourself after learning about
your universal support?

Reminders

Create your reminders below

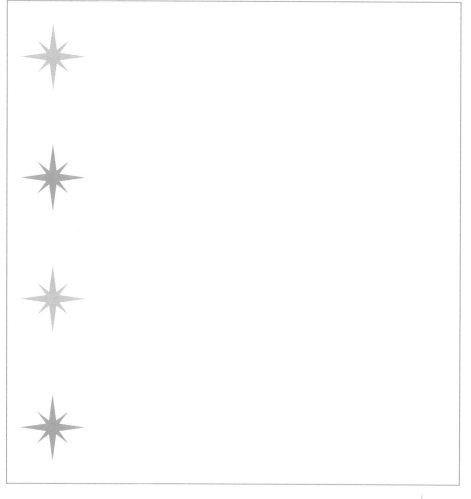

*I acknowledge you today
for your presence.
You learned what universal support
is for the well-being of your mind,
body, and spirit.
I invite you to appreciate yourself
right now, in this moment.
As you begin to implement this new
choreography into your daily
routine, know how grateful your
body feels and what else is
possible right now.*

Shine On

Gina

Intentional Expression

41

Dear Dancer,

I know what it's like to be a high achiever while taking class and struggle with clear communication as you are striving to set loving boundaries and honor your body first.

I know what it's like to think about what to say and when to say things as you discover there is not enough time during class and even in between class to organize your thoughts.

I also know that as you discover what intentional expression is for you in the following pages, you will begin to understand how to communicate easily and effectively.

You will start to notice how simple your verbal and written communication skills will shine and how easy it will be to express yourself in a hurry.

I know in this moment, your self talk is creating a new line of communication to your body, as you will practice this intentional expression choreography.

So, are you ready to turn the page and step onto the well-being stage? A 5678... *Gina*

Intentional Expression

Intentional Expression is being aware and mindful of the words, thoughts, and actions you are saying, thinking, and communicating.

Fill in the blank:

Intentional expression for me is...

Self-Assessment

On a scale of 1–10, 10 being the best, color in the number that reflects your understanding of what intentional expression is right now?

What is a specific action you can choose that will encourage you to move forward to the next number?

On a scale of 1–10, 10 being the best, color in the number that reflects your intentional expression right now?

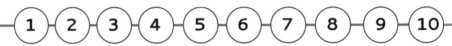

What is a specific action you can choose that will encourage you to move forward to the next number?

On a scale of 1–10, 10 being the best, color in the number that reflects your willingness to learn about your intentional expression?

1 2 3 4 5 6 7 8 9 10

What is a specific action you can choose that will encourage you to move forward to the next number?

Professional Tips

Dr. Stella

"Today as I open this door, I open myself up to new possibilities with ease. As I close this door behind me, I leave this space with appreciation and gratitude "

For every movement you make,
ask what is my intention?

Karen Turnbull

Stretch your arms wide, breathe deeply in through the nose and exhale through the mouth slowly.
Repeat 3 times.

Take your fingers to your scalp and give it a massage.

Self-Caring

Gina's Self-Caring Shares

- Each day I say "May my words create mutual understanding and love towards myself and others"

- I text and email when I am in my highest vibration only

- I project love and possabilities towards others even when its challenging

Next to each bullet, fill in the blank

- Each day I say "

- I text and email when

- I project

Self-Awareness

What is one thing you learned about yourself after taking the self-assessment?

What is one specific skill or action from your self-assessment that you will implement today?

What professional tip will you begin to use?

What will you choose from the self caring worksheet to take action on?

What will your life look, feel, and sound like if you decide to use your self-awareness tools?

Self-Reflection

What do you know now about your intentional expression that you did not know before this workbook?

On a scale of 1-10, 10 being the best, color in the number that best reflects your confidence now about your intentional expression?

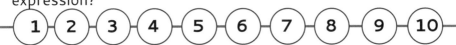

What is a specific skill or action you will begin to practice for your intentional expression?

What reminder will encourage you to remember what your intentional expression is?

What do you appreciate about yourself after learning about your intentional expression?

Reminders

Create your reminders below

I acknowledge you today for your loving words.
You learned what intentional expression is for the well-being of your mind, body, and spirit.
I invite you to appreciate yourself right now, in this moment.
As you begin to implement this new choreography into your daily routine, know how grateful your body feels and what else is possible right now.

Shine On

Gina

Conscious
Fuel

Dear Dancer,

I know what it's like to be a high performing artist, and still feel unclear on how to fuel the body properly, as you move from class to class so quickly.

I know what it's like to think about when and how one would get to fuel adequately, as you want to feel confident in your fuel choices, so you can feel secure in your body movements and honor what your body requires.

I also know that as you discover what conscious fuel is for you in the following pages, you will begin to enjoy cooking your conscious snacks and knowing what to purchase at the grocery store.

You will start to notice how simple fueling your mind, body, and spirit is, and how much better your mind, body, and spirit will feel.

I know right now, you are curious about conscious fuel, and I know you will practice this conscious fuel choreography

So, are you ready to turn the page and step onto the well-being stage? A 5678... *Gina*

Conscious Fuel

Conscious fuel is being aware of what
you are choosing to put in your mind,
body, and spirit.

Fill in the blank:

Conscious Fuel for me is...

Self-Assessment

On a scale of 1–10, 10 being the best, color in the number that reflects your understanding of what conscious fuel is right now?

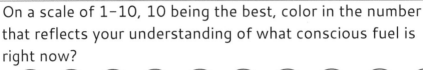

What is a specific action you can choose that will encourage you to move forward to the next number?

On a scale of 1–10, 10 being the best, color in the number that reflects your conscious fuel right now?

What is a specific action you can choose that will encourage you to move forward to the next number?

On a scale of 1–10, 10 being the best, color in the number that reflects your willingness to learn about your conscious fuel?

What is a specific action you can choose that will encourage you to move forward to the next number?

Professional Tips

Dr. Stella

Find foods, books, and audios, that expand
you and light you up.

Ask yourself, "What food and drink am I putting in
my body, who and what am I listening to, does it
expand me or contract me?

Karen Turnbull

Eat the rainbow! The beautiful colors of vegetables are
due to the different vitamins and minerals they
contain.

Protein is needed to repair and rebuild the muscle tissue.
Healthy carbohydrates fuel your energy

Self-Caring

Gina's Self-Caring Shares

- I muscle test my body to decide what drink and foods my body wants each day

- I choose whole foods

- I make sure my purse and or travel bag has the snacks and minerals I need to keep my body fueled properly

Next to each bullet, fill in the blank

- In order to know what food and drink my body wants I choose

- I choose to

- I make sure my purse or travel bag has

Self-Awareness

What is one thing you learned about yourself after taking the self-assessment?

What is one specific skill or action from your self-assessment that you will implement today?

What professional tip will you begin to use?

What will you choose from the self caring worksheet to take action on?

What will your life look, feel, and sound like if you decide to use your self-awareness tools?

Self-Reflection

What do you know now about your conscious fuel
that you did not know before this workbook?

On a scale of 1-10, 10 being the best, color in the number that
best reflects your confidence now about your conscious fuel?

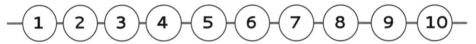

What is a specific skill or action you will begin to practice for
your conscious fuel?

What reminder will encourage you to remember what
consciously fuels you?

What do you appreciate about yourself after learning about
your conscious fuel?

Reminders

Create your reminders below

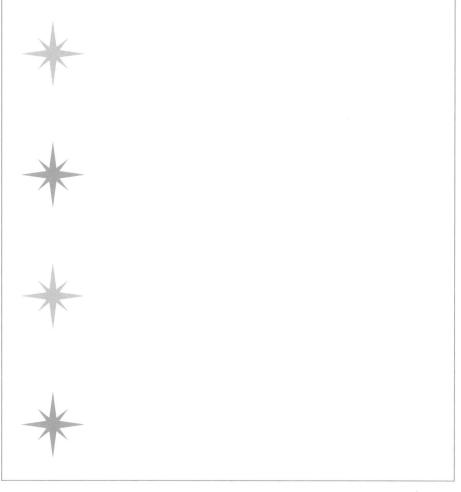

I acknowledge you today for your awareness.
You learned what conscious fuel is for the well–being of your mind, body, and spirit.
I invite you to appreciate yourself right now, in this moment.
As you begin to implement this new choreography into your daily routine, know how grateful your body feels and what else is possible right now.

Shine On

Gina

Balanced Brain

Dear Dancer,

I know what it's like to be a high performing artist, and still feel emotionally and physically unbalanced, as your dance choreography keeps you in 24/7 thinking mode.

I know what it's like to think, and think, and think, as you think, that thinking is the correct way to retain the choreography and you really want to know how to relax your mind.

I also know that as you learn how to take time, because you have time, to create space inside your mind and body connection, you will begin to feel present and peaceful.

You will start to notice how much better you can retain your choreography and how much better you feel in your mind and body.

I know in this moment, you are awaiting your balanced brain choreography so you know exactly your steps to being in balance, which is presence.

So, are you ready to turn the page and step onto the well-being stage? A 5678...

Gina

Balanced Brain

Balanced brain is creating an internal and external environment that allows your brain to function optimally.

Fill in the blank:

Balanced brain for me is...

Self-Assessment

On a scale of 1–10, 10 being the best, color in the number that reflects your understanding of what balanced brain is right now?

What is a specific action you can choose that will encourage you to move forward to the next number?

On a scale of 1–10, 10 being the best, color in the number that reflects your balanced brain right now?

What is a specific action you can choose that will encourage you to move forward to the next number?

On a scale of 1–10, 10 being the best, color in the number that reflects your willingness to learn about your balanced brain?

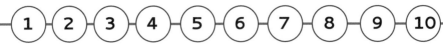

What is a specific action you can choose that will encourage you to move forward to the next number?

Professional Tips

Dr. Stella

> Find time to walk in nature and away from technology and stand on a wobble board to improve balance.

> Eat fats that fuel the brain, like avocado, nuts, extra virgin olive oil, and coconut oil.

Karen Turnbull

> Hydration is essential

> Take a short gentle walk outside to increase circulation and oxygen flow to the brain. Breathe gently and steadily as you walk

Self-Caring

Gina's Self-Caring Shares

- I choose three to five brain resets a day

- I schedule appointments once a month to get my brain professionally balanced

- I am mindful of feeding and hydrating my brain properly

Next to each bullet, fill in the blank

- I choose to reset my brain by

- I schedule

- I am mindful of

Self-Awareness

What is one thing you learned about yourself after taking the self-assessment?

What is one specific skill or action from your self-assessment that you will implement today?

What professional tip will you begin to use?

What will you choose from the self caring worksheet to take action on?

What will your life look, feel, and sound like if you decide to use your self-awareness tools?

Self-Reflection

What do you know now about your balanced brain
that you did not know before this workbook?

On a scale of 1–10, 10 being the best, color in the number that
best reflects your confidence now about your balanced brain?

What is a specific skill or action you will begin to practice for
your balanced brain?

What reminder will encourage you to remember what
balances your brain?

What do you appreciate about yourself after learning about
your balanced brain?

Reminders

Create your reminders below

I acknowledge you today for your compassion.
You learned what a balanced brain is for the well-being of your mind, body, and spirit.
I invite you to appreciate yourself right now, in this moment.
As you begin to implement this new choreography into your daily routine, know how grateful your body feels and what else is possible right now.

Shine On

Gina

Embodied Energy

Dear Dancer,

I know what it's like to be a high achieving soul, and still feel anxious and stressed, as you are feeling the need to push your body in every direction keeping you stuck in fight or flight mode instead of rest and relax mode.

I know what it's like to want to feel calm and clear inside your mind and body, and yet be unaware of how to access that inner calm as you are on the go, go, go.

I also know that as you learn how to tune into the energy you want to feel, and easily raise your vibration, you will be so grateful that you can still accomplish all you want to by listening to the wisdom of your body so clearly.

You will begin to understand the law of attraction, and begin to create the life you really really want, with ease and with joy, while hearing what is highest and best for you.

I know that as you start to be aware of energy, you will begin to feel self-assured in your embodied energy choreography practice.

So, are you ready to turn the page and step onto the well-being stage? A 5678... *Gina*

Embodied Energy

Embodied energy is choosing the energy that fuels your body to function in a state of well-being.

Fill in the blank:

Embodied Energy for me is...

Self-Assessment

On a scale of 1–10, 10 being the best, color in the number that reflects your understanding of what embodied energy is right now?

What is a specific action you can choose that will encourage you to move forward to the next number?

On a scale of 1–10, 10 being the best, color in the number that reflects your embodied energy right now?

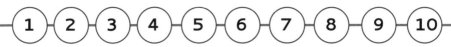

What is a specific action you can choose that will encourage you to move forward to the next number?

On a scale of 1–10, 10 being the best, color in the number that reflects your willingness to learn about your embodied energy?

What is a specific action you can choose that will encourage you to move forward to the next number?

Professional Tips

Dr. Stella

The words you say have energy, The thoughts you think have energy.

What energy are you sending out to you and others? Is it love, appreciation, and gratitude or something else?

Karen Turnbull

Think of your body as an energy savings account. Deposit whole foods from the earth and feel your investment grow!

Create this imaginary bubble around you filled with love and light.

Self-Caring

Gina's Self-Caring Shares

- My morning routine is filled with meditation, grounding, and raising my vibration

- I choose to use, one of my favorite tools, gold star

- I choose people, places, and things that are a match in the energy I want to feel

Next to each bullet, fill in the blank

- My morning routine is filled with

- My favorite way to embody my energy is

- I choose people, places, and things that

Self-Awareness

What is one thing you learned about yourself after taking the self-assessment?

What is one specific skill or action from your self-assessment that you will implement today?

What professional tip will you begin to use?

What will you choose from the self caring worksheet to take action on?

What will your life look, feel, and sound like if you decide to use your self-awareness tools?

Self-Reflection

What do you know now about your embodied energy that you did not know before this workbook?

On a scale of 1-10, 10 being the best, color in the number that best reflects your confidence now about your embodied energy?

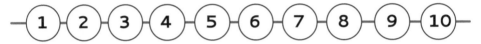

What is a specific skill or action you will begin to practice for your embodied energy?

What reminder will encourage you to remember what embodies your energy?

What do you appreciate about yourself after learning about your embodied energy?

78

Reminders

Create your reminders below

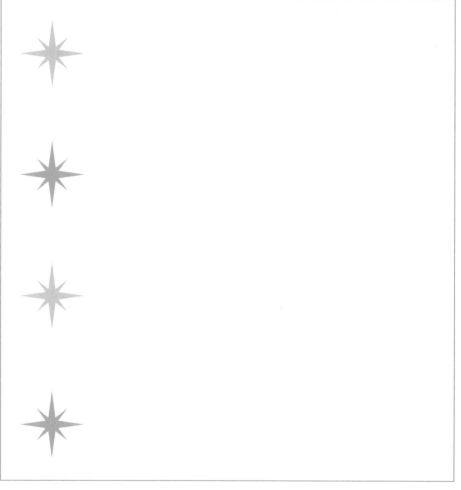

*I acknowledge you today for being
aware your energy.
You learned what embodied energy
is for the well-being of your mind,
body, and spirit.
I invite you to appreciate yourself
right now, in this moment.
As you begin to implement this new
choreography into your daily
routine, know how grateful your
body feels and what else is
possible right now.*

Shine On

Gina

Resources

Dear Dancer,

YOU DID IT!! You finished Your Claim Your Confidence Workbook and now you know exactly what your mind, body, and spirit choreography is to Embrace Your Well-Being. (Applause)

In this moment, you now know what your body requires each day in mind, body, and spirit. (Applause)

You know how to be a 4 on the self-assessment scale, and move forward to a 10, and keep moving forward each day. (Applause)

You see dancing soul, confidence is not about being a 10 all the time, or finishing the tasks each day, or even receiving the awards... (although those feel GREAT!)

It is about knowing the extraordinary human being you are today, in your mind, your body, and your spirit. It is knowing what you love, the people you get to share life with, and your path towards well-being each day.

I shared in my introduction that what you choose to repeat in your mind, your body, and your spirit creates your life.

So, are you ready to turn the page and step onto the well-being stage? I have provided daily resources for you to master your daily well-being choreography, daily. (HA!) A 5678...

Gina

Daily Resources

- Visual Chart

- Self–Caring Checklist

- Picture Board

- Daily Self–Assessment

- Daily Self Reflection

- Gina's Minute to Win It Tools

- Letter to Self

5678,
You
Got This!

Visual Chart

Visual Chart

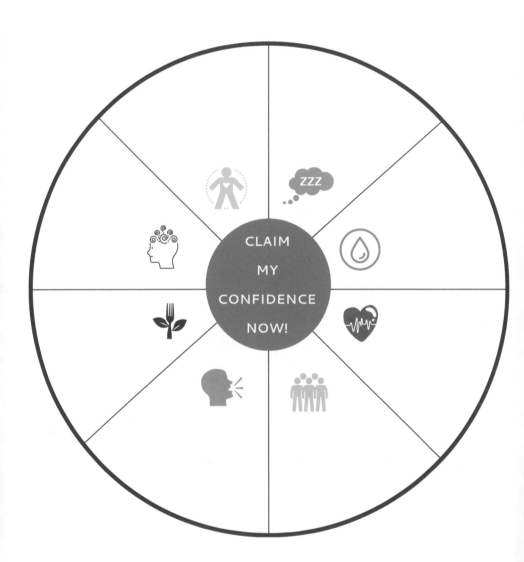

Self-Caring Checklist

Picture Board

A Picture Board or Vision creates an
image to support your soul's direction

Create your picture board below by drawing, writing,
images, or writing choosing your
8 Step to Embrace Your Well-Being

Picture Board

$\mathscr{Self}$ ASSESSMENT

- On a scale of 1–10, 10 being the best, color in the number that reflects your restful sleep today?

What action can you choose to move you forward one number?

- On a scale of 1–10, 10 being the best, color in the number that reflects your mindful hydration right now?

What action can you choose to move you forward one number?

- On a scale of 1–10, 10 being the best, color in the number that reflects your empowered heart right now?

What action can you choose to move you forward one number?

- On a scale of 1–10, 10 being the best, color in the number that reflects your universal support today now?

What action can you choose to move you forward one number?

$\mathcal{Self}$ ASSESSMENT

- On a scale of 1–10, 10 being the best, color in the number that reflects your intentional expression right now?

What action can you choose to move you forward one number?

- On a scale of 1–10, 10 being the best, color in the number that reflects your conscious fuel right now?

What action can you choose to move you forward one number?

- On a scale of 1–10, 10 being the best, color in the number that reflects your balanced brain right now?

What action can you choose to move you forward one number?

- On a scale of 1–10, 10 being the best, color in the number that reflects your embodied energy right now?

What action can you choose to move you forward one number?

Self REFLECTION

WHAT IS MY SELF AWARENESS TODAY?

WHAT DID I LEARN TODAY THAT CAN BENEFIT MY WELL-BEING?

WHAT THREE THINGS DO I APPRECIATE THE MOST TODAY?

Minute to Win It

Espresso Shot

Inhale through the nose slowly, hold it for 2 counts, then exhale through the mouth slowly

Gold Star

Step into a wide second position, lift your arms into a high 'V', open your jazz hands, smile so bright, and light yourself up like a gold star

Right Now Tool

Right Now, (fill in the blank)
Right now, I am writing this tool for the readers.
Right now, I am wearing my Presence, Passion, Purpose tank top.

Hi Body!

Say, "Hi body, hi mind, hi heart, any and all energies that do not belong to me, I ask to return their owner with light and love."

Appreciation

"I am aware, right now I appreciate my health. I am aware, right now I appreciate you reading this. I am aware right now, I appreciate my gifts." Thank You.

Letter to Self

Write a letter to yourself in the present moment of what you know right now.
Example: Dear Gina, I know right now I wrote a workbook for dancers. I know right now I am a former Radio City Rockette. I know right now I love dance.

Thank You!

"I acknowledge and appreciate this journey with you. Remember, the path can be filled with ease, joy, grace, and fun. The possibilities that are for you, will show up for you, in your timing. I honor this moment with you and celebrate your 8 Steps to Embracing your Well-Being."
Welcome to Your Style of Confidence!

With loving support and light,

Gina

Scan me

www.ginapero.com

Made in the USA
Columbia, SC
28 July 2024

39106750R00061